# When Ancient Starlight Falls to Earth

## Songs and Poems

### Caitlín Matthews

APOCRYPHILE
PRESS

Apocryphile Press
PO Box 255
Hannacroix, NY 12087
www.apocryphilepress.com

Copyright © 2026 by Caitlín Matthews
Printed in the United States of America
ISBN 978-1-965646-61-8 | paper
ISBN 978-1-965646-62-5 | ePub

Cover image: Christine and the Sybil pointing to a ladder from the heavens, from the Book of the Queen, France (Paris), c. 1410–1414, Harley MS 4431, f. 189v. Harley MS 4431, f. 189v.png British Museum.

The back image of Caitlín Matthews bearing the attributes of Rhiannon was painted by Nicole Ni Riain in 1986.

No part of this book may be reproduced, stored in a retrieval system, or transmitted in any form or by any means—electronic, mechanical, photocopy, recording, or otherwise —without written permission of the author and publisher, except for brief quotations in printed reviews.

Please join our mailing list at www.apocryphilepress.com/free. We'll keep you up-to—date on all our new releases, and we'll also send you a FREE BOOK. Visit us today!

# CONTENTS

Acknowledgments ix
Preface xi

## SONGS
Brightest Stars 3
Nehalennia the Steerswoman 4
Orkney Song 5
Sacred Companions 7
The Hyperboreans 9
Troytown Song 11
Song of the Spheres 13

## SEASONS
Hallowe'en Story 17
Hearth Song 19
Snow Day 21
Blessing of the Rain 23

## OCCASIONS
Dawn Watch 27
Out of the Workhouse 29
An Expostulation Upon AI 31
An Ode to Oxford Physicke 33

## DREAMS
Dream Deep Awake 37
The Hills Call Out 39
Seven Singing Birds 41

## LOVE
Heloise to Abelard 45
Love's Invasion 47
Three Feathers 48

| | |
|---|---|
| I Have a Light | 51 |
| Beauty and the Beast | 53 |
| Verses to John | 57 |
| Within Kabalistic Memory | 61 |

## MYTHS

| | |
|---|---|
| Myth Land | 65 |
| The Time of Magic | 67 |
| Where Three Cranes Fly at Dawn | 69 |
| Homeward the Heroes | 71 |
| The Myth is Yet Living | 73 |
| Minotaur | 75 |
| Essential Mythologies | 77 |
| A Green Killing | 79 |
| Written in Gold | 83 |
| Arthur Wakens Everywhere | 85 |
| Survivors of Camlann | 87 |

## DIVINITIES & SPIRITS

| | |
|---|---|
| Daimonic Sequence | 95 |
| The Old Woman of Beare | 99 |
| Sovereignty's Challenge | 101 |
| Feast of the Queen of Snows | 103 |

## PRAYERS

| | |
|---|---|
| Prayer of the Birds | 107 |
| I Shall Take Poetry as My Prayer | 109 |
| Nomad's Prayer | 111 |
| Bone Song | 113 |
| Spell-Song to Restore the Earth | 115 |

## PEOPLE

| | |
|---|---|
| Companions in the Dark | 119 |
| The Lantern Bearer | 121 |
| He Was Made Music | 125 |
| To Her Secret Bower | 129 |

## PLACES & JOURNEYS

| | |
|---|---|
| Farewell, You Bright Dancers | 133 |
| Beyond the Ninth Wave | 135 |
| Bhalasaigh Sunset | 137 |
| Sea-Master | 139 |
| Bosham Sequence | 141 |

## VISIONS

| | |
|---|---|
| Sea Lanterns | 147 |
| In Praise of Darkness | 149 |
| In Dazzling Darkness | 151 |
| Cleave to Your Star | 153 |
| Eternally Engraved | 155 |
| Chant of the Ancestors | 156 |
| | |
| Poetic Contexts | 157 |
| | |
| About the Author | 167 |

*For John, my companion in all things.*

---

*'In his loneliness and fixedness,
he yearneth towards the journeying Moon,
and the stars that still sojourn,
yet still move onwards;
and everywhere the blue sky belongs to them,
and is their appointed rest,
and their native country and their own natural homes,
which they enter unannounced,
as lords that are certainly expected,
and yet there is a silent joy at their arrival.'*

*—from "The Rime of the Ancient Mariner"
by Samuel Taylor Coleridge:*

# ACKNOWLEDGMENTS

Many of these poems have appeared in different places but none have been collected together before. *Poetry London, Temenos, Hampshire Poets, Labrys* and others have hosted some of their appearances, while invididual poems have made one-off visitations within my own books since 1984. My songs have been heard by many, and a few of them can be heard on my album, *Deep Well In the Wildwood*. Many thanks go to John Mabry for kindly publishing this collection. See p. 157 for the key to poetic context of each poem.

# PREFACE
## BETWEEN THE THRESHOLDS OF THE WORLDS

For me, song has always come first, since I was singing before I was speaking. Poetry and spontaneous song with words bear a very close relationship in my family of utterances and writings, which is also why I have been serially employed in the walking-between-the-worlds arts of vatic and divinatory skill most of my life. In my shamanic practice still, I sing for my clients the songs that are arising from their soul-landscape: songs that I do not know but which are ever arising; these are songs that I cannot sing or capture again, for they remain only with the client as reminders of who and where they are. My twin images of these comings forth of poems and songs are of ancient starlight falling to the earth, and also of underground water coming to the surface—I experience both these kinds of inspiration. The mysterious sending of poetry comes either as an invocation or an evocation of what lies beyond our immediate reach.

These otherworlds of knowing reveal themselves in the moment, often translating the momentary experience into the captivation of enchantment; for there the portal opens revealing, in a fraction of time, the eternal moment that seizes or illumines the soul. Here the truth of myth—which is the truest thing that ever was or will be—

# PREFACE

reconnects me with the ongoing and perpetual understanding of Wisdom, the goddess whom I have ever served. It is no mistake that the *Orphic Hymns* begin with lines like 'Attend, O Muses, to my sacred song, and learn what rites to sacrifice belong.' Or, 'With Holy Voice I call the Stars on high, pure sacred lights and genii of the sky,' in the translation of Thomas Taylor. Yes, spirits come upon the wings of the song, but they can also speak and sing through the voice of the poet or practitioner, becoming oracles to those who are gathered for ritual, and as reminders to look up and about us for our own portals and messengers.

These precious arts cannot be co-opted to corporate usage, as many a poet laureate has discovered, because they are the freely-given gift of a moment: and while occasional poems may be requested, they usually only show themselves when *they* want, and not when so commanded. Yet it is also the poet's task to reveal the true context at the crossroads of history, where decisions that change the world are undertaken. Bearing witness to the macrocosmic view is a duty at a time where these precious arts are often seen as redundant. They ensure that we do not become sealed into one side of reality without that cynosure into the greater world, that we remember both ancestral heritage and responsibility to the descendants. May we still sing our songs to remind everyone of Gerard Manley Hopkins' conviction, that there still 'lives the deep down freshness deep down things.' We cannot live with them.

*Caitlín Matthews*
*25<sup>th</sup> October 2025*
*Oxford.*

# SONGS

# BRIGHTEST STARS

Brightest stars disclose their blessing,
Night folds fast the welcome dream.
Thoughts go free of all distressing,
Waken to the greater scheme.

Where our joys spring up triumphant,
Where our dreams run to the sea.
May the keeper of the dreaming,
Blessings send to you and me.

# Nehalennia the Steerswoman

Wanderers, Wayfarers, Travellers over,
Over the seas, and over the flood.
Pilgrims and migrants upon all the pathways,
Across every threshold I carry you through.

Souls in migration and winged ones who wander,
Over the skyways you roam without star,
A chart I will lend you, to guide and direct you,
The dream-ways unlocking that you may go far!

# ORKNEY SONG

While I am here, I just want to be golden,
Golden as no-one before me has been.
Stolen from busyness, absent from sorrow,
Open to sun-spells, woken to dream.

Let the sun wake me to lake's bright devotion,
A bird who is learning to feather its wings.
Cleansed by clear waters, the charm is swung open—
The long-silent blessing I'm able to sing.

Mystical morning, you've fathomed the meaning
Behind all the bustle that catches the tune.
Shaken on farmstead and hill-distant dwelling,
Showing how shadow reveals the lost rune.

Now that I sing with the voice of the ancients,
I can fly higher, right into the sun.
Barring my wings with the blessing of brightness,
Golden I'll be till the singing is done.

# SACRED COMPANIONS

You are gathering from the times between,
Companions of the brave,
Assembling on the plains of history.
And the spirits gleam within your eyes
To show us all the way,
Your feet in shoes of bronze
From oceans far.

Sacred companions,
Shoal on this shore.
Bring us the beauty,
That we still adore.
Dance for the daylight
Sing for the shore,
Keep bright the loving
And we'll dance once more.

Your sea-washed bodies come to praise
The ancient memories' store,
Hidden deep within the sands beyond the bay.

# WHEN ANCIENT STARLIGHT FALLS TO EARTH

You're still shining out the story,
Blessings of the Ever-Young,
Wine for all to drink,
For we who follow on.

Sacred companions,
Gathering here.
Show us horizons
Where we shall not fear.
Unfurl the sail now,
Chart us the track,
Give us a way now
That we can sail back.

Through the tides of time the waters flow,
Seasons dance their yearly round,
Ancient stories blend with new ones every day;
But the sacred inspirations
From the heart of all we've known,
Guide the paths our children tread
When we are gone.

Sacred companions,
Loved from before,
Welcome you show us
When we learn your lore:
Make bright our hearts now,
Teach us the song,
Play for our dancing,
That souls may be strong.

# THE HYPERBOREANS

Over the ocean an island there lies
Under the shield of the Bear,
Hyperboreans inhabit that isle
Beyond where the north wind does blow.

>   *Chorus*: Neither by ship nor on foot will you find
>   The marvelous road to the place where they gather.

Leto the Lady was born in that land,
They honour her son every one of their days.
Apollo the Hyperborean they sing,
In their daily, perpetual praise.

Sacred his city, upon the wide plain,
A spherical precinct of stones,
And offerings many adorning that ring
Where Apollo himself goes dancing

Nor illness nor age are within their sweet blood,
As far from all labour and battle their singing.
The muse with her lyre, the maidens' own dance
Are calling you here from afar.

> *Chorus*: Neither by ship nor on foot will you find
> The marvelous road of the Hyperboreans.

# TROYTOWN SONG

Come and join your glad voices unto our old song,
To raise up the walls of the Troytown so strong;
For the love of the dancing, we bid you all sing,
For the true light of summer is the burden we bring.

Come and raise up
Come and raise up
Come and raise up
The old Troytown this day.

Come and raise your glad voices both strong, loud and clear
Come and join in the old mazey way without fear;
For the summer's come in and the winter's away,
And we bid you make merry this midsummer day.

Come and be joined
Come and be joined
Come and be joined
To the Troytown this day.

# TROYTOWN SONG

For the love of our Saviour who died on the tree,
And the halt and the blind that he made for to see,
Of your mercy, we bid you come out of your door
And witness the midsummer dancing once more.

Come and be blessed
Come and be blessed
Come and be blessed
By the Troytown this day.

May the blessings of God be upon your young ones,
And the old folks and servants and masters and sons,
May the beasts of the byre and the fish in the sea,
Make plentiful harvest for you and for me.

Welcome this day
Welcome this day
Welcome this day
Is the old mazey way.

Here's a health to the Dod Man and his Lady Wife!
Here's a health to their children and a long happy life!
Here's a health to the maiden who spins by the fire!
And a drop of good cider for the dancers who tire!

Raise us all up
Raise us all up
Raise us all up
With the old cider cup!

# SONG OF THE SPHERES

The spindle it is turning,
Turning between the knees of Night,
Her own three daughters yearning,
For the fate of the thread so bright.

And the siren voices singing,
Each voice about the eight-spun whorl,
Eight pure star-notes they are ringing,
A single harmony of pearl.

Lachesis notes the passing,
Clotho weaves the present web,
Atropos notes the coming,
Of the eight-fold gifted thread.

Turn, O turn, the whorl of singing,
Let us know each gifting star,
Learn, O learn, the song's beginning,
We remember from afar.

## SONG OF THE SPHERES

Selene brings us sleeping,
Helios brings the gift of mirth,
Aphrodite's heart is keeping,
Hermes carries speech to earth.

Ares' fire is the kindling,
Zeus the life-breath of each birth,
Cronos brings the gift of grieving,
To all mortals bound for earth.

But the radiant lady shining,
Queen of every blessed night:
Urania's constellating,
Keeping harmony arright.

She the wisdom of our weaving,
Sings the planets to their rest:
She the octave, she the reiving
Goddess of each mortal guest.

# SEASONS

# HALLOWE'EN STORY

On every hedge the ivy shines,
The winds increase, the sun declines;
Branches go bare, woods full of care,
And so do I.

Streams run bright with steely rain;
Lungs scarce draw their breath from pain;
Sheep from their fold, gorse sheds its gold,
And so do I.

The sledge of story slips its load,
The wheels of myth run off the road;
Thoughts grow grey, love goes astray,
And do I.

Clouds whip All Hallows to the skies,
Forebears awake with ghastly cries;
Furious the burn, the green leaves turn,
And so do I.

# WHEN ANCIENT STARLIGHT FALLS TO EARTH

Take now the broom and sweep away
The remnant of the long-gone day.
Fire takes the spark, ancestors hark,
And so do I.

Fresh tales about the fire are told,
Myths reinspire both young and old.
The lean years quake, new years awake,
And so do I.

# HEARTH SONG

Bring in more logs, the day grows chill!
It's time to gather round the fire.
Across the fields, the snow lies still,
The beasts lie safely in warm byre.

When wind blows down the chimney steep,
And red-gold sparks leap in the dark,
It's time to open the book of story,
And learn of winter's hidden glory.

Peer in the blaze: where elf-caves glow,
Where dragons breathe and beanstalks grow;
Where lost companions find their way,
Where jewels and secret treasures lay,

To hear what has been told before
By those who sat in times long past,
Round fires where children begged for more:
'Don't let this story be the last!'

## WHEN ANCIENT STARLIGHT FALLS TO EARTH

And still in winters yet to come,
When starlight sings the snowflakes' song,
When moon is bright and dull is sun,
And all these tales to you belong,

Remember then this winter night,
When snow lay thick and wind blew cold.
Tell the glad tales round hearth-fire's light,
For your own children to have and hold.

# SNOW DAY

The words come tumbling in without a doubt:
'The day's dawned white, refreshed and young,'
—Snow's in my open, wondering mouth.

News of the snow, the busy traffic's rout
(Waking at six, breath in the still air hung,)
The words come tumbling in without a doubt,

Children take up this morning's thankful shout:
Tidings I bring upon my eager tongue,
Snow's in my open, wondering mouth.

Gentling the heart of every city lout,
Snowballs turn the kill-joy Scrooge-cop's gun;
The words come tumbling in without a doubt.

Gather together with a gladsome shout!
Carolling sweetly, let old songs be sung:
Tunes from my open, wondering mouth.

## SNOW DAY

Christmas is come, snow's secret is furled out,
Bells bright the hills, with laughter swung,
The words come tumbling in without a doubt:
Snow's in my open, wondering mouth.

# BLESSING OF THE RAIN
## RORATE COELI DE SUPER

Rain holds its breath, then pelts the window clean:
The headlong hurtle of the shower comes down.
Men who have altered cells are now asleep,
But barren women waken to the rain.

Now you are claiming all your heart has held,
All in the shelter of a summer night.
There is no brightness like the dew of hearts:
Tears that in darkness heal love's old deceits;
The voided promises that lovers left,
Gather like hopeful creatures beyond bars.

Scratching at scars, women grow fair by dream.
A new complexion curtains pain from sight,
And all the unnumbering stars draw close to sing
A new creation as the dew drops down.

After long dryness, seeds unfurl at root,
Germs of a generation, spirit-sown.
Rice-grains of rain engender on the glass

## BLESSING OF THE RAIN

And in the deep alembic of the womb.
Alchemical imaginings run free
In men weary of dessicate, lonely hours.

Beyond window's blackness stirs life's urgent shoot:
Go down to the dark to greet its bliss once more,
Wrapped in the veil of waters, scattering dew,
Seeking the chance-come lover of the hour.

Now you are blessing every star you kissed,
Risking the old wives' word at every step;
Thigh-deep, the green-gold grains embrace,
Hiding from morning grudge, from doubt's midday.
Here, before harvest, play the ripening game,
Gather up bright seeds from bitter tears.

Rain holds its course, then lets the daylight down.
Dreams that in darkness twined, stretch out their legs.
Men wake with women, to their heart's desire.
Radiant is the jewel-speckled dawn.

# OCCASIONS

# DAWN WATCH
## ON MY MOTHER'S PASSING

Two birds fly up in the dawning
As the darkness turns to gold,
Clouds pass south to the rising tide
Like argosies of old.

With scarce a breath to fill her sails,
She lies in the harbour slack;
Enduring the roll of the petulant shoal,
She waits for the wind to back.

As day dawns pure, night's peace slips out,
The bustle of life speeds on.
Becalmed in a mist that hugs the shore,
Her colours flame, fade, and are gone.

Those who sleep with dread to rise,
Dream fast of the voyage to come.
For the chart tells not where the barque must steer,
Nor how deep the lead might plumb.

# WHEN ANCIENT STARLIGHT FALLS TO EARTH

By unseen star her chart is set,
To unknown seas she steers.
Her goal, desire of shores long-dreamed,
Her freight, the untold years.

The sun comes up with crown of gold;
Her captain cries, 'All hands!'
Two birds as pilots clear the clouds
As she sails to distant lands.

*Portsmouth*

# OUT OF THE WORKHOUSE
## FOR MY PATERNAL GRANDMOTHER, CHARLOTTE STILLWELL, NÉE NEWMAN

In a rough kitchen devoid of beauty,
She sat in a brown deal chair,
A flowered overall about her breasts.
The clock ticked but she never minded the minutes,
For she was in her own kitchen and free:
Free to come and free to go, but now especially,
Free to sit and be, as well she might
Who'd raised five children at her knee.

And every Saturday they visited,
Shouting over each other, arguing
Sport and politics so loud that the dog barked too
And had to be led away to a quiet room.

She sat too when her husband died,
And when she moved to a smaller house,
With only an elderly daughter for company,
But now she sat in the front room,
Graduated from the kitchen's theatre
To the royal box, surrounded by tokens

## WHEN ANCIENT STARLIGHT FALLS TO EARTH

Of trips to Scotland and abroad.

She sat and never said what kept her quiet,
Remembering the day when she and her family
Entered the workhouse after her father died,
When they pulled off the soft woollen dress
Her mother had made and clothed her in workhouse grey,
With scratchy collar and close bonnet
And gave her tasks would last all day.
Gruel and soup, bread and cheese
Cut thin and eaten by rote,
A little meat or bacon twice a week
And the hard meanness wearing love away.

At thirteen when she ceased to be a
Pauper scholar, she passed beyond those doors,
Glad to clean the butcher's block and floor,
To taste the city air and sit idle on Sundays.
She owed no-one, and no-one could touch her,
Save death, a welcome guest now.
When she lay down last in the front room,
It was with open arms, pushing wide
The workhouse doors for all who cried alone.

# AN EXPOSTULATION UPON AI

They call it artificial, for a start.
It is certainly not intelligent,
Unless mirrors can be so called.
It scrapes and copies,
By theft and subtle craft.
Unasked and uninvited,
It has grasped just enough
To think itself indispensable,
But lacks the charm
To claim our hearts.

Never trust a voice that that cannot sing lullabies,
Nor a brain that cannot remember experience.
AI has never been in a body:
Never had hands to stroke or slap it,
Never hidden in a bush or lain on a hillside
To hear the lark's soaring song.
It has never given birth,
Nor been stung by a thistle,
It has never been done a wrong.

## WHEN ANCIENT STARLIGHT FALLS TO EARTH

When it has known anxiety,
When it has been bitten by necessity,
When it has suffered loss,
And wailed all night from pain,
When it has had to take responsibility,
Tell it to call again.
Until then...

...Let it read x-rays,
Find anomalies medics might miss;
Let it virtually unroll the unread
Carbonized scrolls of Herculaneum.
Keep it far from the dear creative kiss
Of mind and heart,
Where poetry and story start.

# AN ODE TO OXFORD PHYSICKE
## WITH APOLOGIES TO DAN CHAUCER

In Aprile, whan shours swote their mercy send, (*sweet showers*)
Whanne man and maid both forth agin would wend,
Comes Oxford Physicke to doth us all delighte.
It cometh to our naked armes arright,
As Mercurie his power, with wand ootstretched,
Oon sharpen pricke, then 'Ouche,' eche one expressed.
So daintily made sooth with healing might;
And forth the miscreant plague is outlawed quite.

Now, as you wenden forth with chariots' race,
To seeke bright Phoebus solace in eche place,
Goo gently, as you drain the foaming caske,
Amid the taverners wear well thy maske.
As once thou sicke did lie, none succour came,
So thinke on those that lyen sick the same!
Remember eke the cunning leechcraft folk,
Who laboured oft when death was alle forespoke.

## AN ODE TO OXFORD PHYSICKE

Beseeche you mercy, alle go sickerer anon,
   *(all will go more certainly soon)*
In goodly cheere now waxen everyone.
Eche man his occupation shall renew,
The gentil mistress shall hir garden sow,
Aged grandsires and their dames may take delighte
In grand-childer that playen fair and bright.
Now welcome somer with thy sparkling ray,
That all our swevens black burn quite away! *(bad dreams)*

# DREAMS

# DREAM DEEP AWAKE

Dream deep, dream deep awake
The lives that live abiding still within.
Only by dreaming can the barrier break
That keeps us closeted within our skin.

Tend the uncared-for silence, like a cloak
Wrap it fast round you in the marketplace,
Lest the fast-flowing song turn into oak,
The uncharted pathway vanish without trace.

Cast the grey circle of your blessing round,
That none may mark the chanter at its heart,
Nor heed the bee-hum of the circled ground
Where spirits wait the whirling dances' start.

# THE HILLS CALL OUT

The hills call out in the morning
Over the fields of frost,
As a pale and brilliant dawning
Ransoms the dreams we've lost.

Aerial tracks of travel
Score the wakening sky.
The primal knots unravel,
Revealing where thresholds lie.

The ancient wisdoms hearken
To present prayers of pain.
And minds and hearts that darken
Are touched by hope again.

The wheel has long been turning
As tides and rivers run;
For wisdom we've been yearning,
For swift return of sun.

By ancient sorrows chastened,
By present woes unstrung,
We call the old ones hasten
To teach us what *they* sung.

Protected be the way-mark
By which our children walk,
Light's benison and its twin, dark,
Shine holy on their talk.

Over this day a glory
Arises once again;
Now *we* shall tell the story
That has no let nor end.

# SEVEN SINGING BIRDS

Seven singing birds fly with me
Their several songs through secret airts
Of heaven make colour, weave sound,
Make bright the taste, fetch smell out of memory,
While each small wingbeat touches deep.

Their tender friendship is my veil and covering
And my earth-walk the points of their flight's
Touchdown where their winged notes spill
New patterns and the wave forms shiver
Upon the hearing ear illimitably.

Veil me ready for flight, mistresses
Of all the arts, make my dance with you
Blessed in every figure, let the song thrill
Each dead darkness to remembrance
Let the spirit-life spring up with glory.

Whether you be with me as seven colours
Seven sounds, seven sisters of pillars

In Wisdom's house standing tall and straight
Be alchemy in me, seven metals sounding
One pure burst of gold forever.

Make harmony of my poor life's music
And instruct the trivium to order, break the
Dense mind-holds with quadrivium
Till I figure every angle, find the
Intersections where life shines out of doubt.

I your laboratory; all my deeds your prayer
Where song is worked and wakened
To macrocosmic choruses of joy.
Seven singing birds fly then with me ever
So the dance can circle onwards.

# LOVE

# HELOISE TO ABELARD

When they cut you, a great sycamore fell in the forest—
Storm-felled wood that they made into a harp.
You will sing again, beloved, never fear!
Only never think that we are parted, for
Where that harp is set to the shoulder,
I am the raised knot in the grain
That can never be planed away.

# LOVE'S INVASION

Love broke in quietly when the chips were down,
When want reduced the walls to rubble;
Ever an opportunist, stealing in by night,
To fill the waiting hollow with no trouble.

Love came to leave a trace, a flavour,
A subtle scent to permeate each place:
An unannounced and unexpected saviour
Invading where no enemy would tread.

No hope of plunder and the pickings slender,
Love brought strange peace, a foreign, homely bread
Whose flavour was familiar and tender,
Filling up neglected absence with strong meat.

# THREE FEATHERS

Three feathers fell from my Borges last night
As I reached for some poems to bring me to rest.
Three feathers turning onto the empty bed—
Swan, goose and duck—still streaked with mud—
From Avon's banks, that Tuesday in October
When we went to Stratford, saw the *Family Reunion*,
And bought books for pleasure:
A day's grace of freedom,
When truth was between us.

And, on the way back,
I read you *The Watcher*—
In his circular cell,
Yoked to his shadow—
And we spoke of how prisoners escape
From the casque and the helmet,
How the story floods back
Like the river whose spate
We once drove through on this very road
Two years ago now,

## THREE FEATHERS

When the prison closed round us
And the darkness made separate
Our cells of unhappiness.

—But there are no prisoners,
And the door is wide open,
And the pit is cleansed
Of its sad ranting figure.
And all days can be that day,
All freedoms desired
Be yours and yours.

And the feathers fell soft
On the place where you sleep—
Duck, goose and swan—
And it never mattered about the mud,
Nor that you slept half a world away,
For the river flows through us
And the feathers we shed
Rest light on the water
Like poetry unsaid.

And I laid the feathers
In formation of flight
On your pillow—
Upon your migrations—
That you may sleep peaceful
And dream back the days of delight.

# I HAVE A LIGHT

I have a light that cannot be put out;
It burns like oil no matter what you do;
So bright it might well set the bed aflame.

It is desired—of that there is no doubt:
Men turn their heads when I go passing by.
I have a light that cannot be put out.

Hungry for the lambent touch of you,
Never needing any fuel but love:
It burns like oil no matter what you do.

Sometimes the glory burns up with a shout,
Trailing sheets of flame that might devour.
I have a light that cannot be put out.

The Pharos of this beacon lights but few,
An altar-flame illumining the wise:
It burns like oil no matter what you do.

## I HAVE A LIGHT

Live in its loving heat and shun self-blame!
I have a light that cannot be put out;
It burns like oil no matter what you do;
So bright it might well set the bed aflame.

# BEAUTY AND THE BEAST

Dinner was always precisely at eight pm.
He appeared joyfully, well-dressed and prompt,
With no expectation. Only a general interest
In what I had done that day.
It did not make him any less horrific, of course.
The horns still skewed over either ear,
The mouth still salivated inconveniently.

Once he showed me Orion after dinner
And the many lesser stars that thronged the heavens.
And, gradually I grew used to his claws on my arm,
The way he turned his head to see
How I was reacting. And, slowly, I began
To love the way he looked into my gaze,
His eyes the hue of bilberries.

After two months of his company at dinner,
I had forgotten to wince when he sucked his teeth,
Or to shudder as his unshapely shadow
Crowded the veranda wall in moonshine.

## BEAUTY AND THE BEAST

I had learned to place my body in the crook
Of his oxter, to perch my chin on his steep chest,
And let my ear rise and fall on the tide of his breath.

And I went reluctantly to my lonely bed
Turning in the silken sheets and sighing
For a thing that I could only guess at.
Dreams of home became nightmares and I woke
With my legs twisted in the foamy covers
And the strong conviction of my father
Lost at sea, like the cargoes that had foundered.

Oh, the long wait till evening to ask his permission
To go home! Oh, he was mild and anxious for me,
Giving me means to travel, making me promise
To look within the magic looking glass
So he could see I was well and happy.
And I left the debatable lands that ringed the estate,
Coming at length to the home I'd been bartered from.

They were all well: step-sisters indifferent,
Though fiercely possessive of the gifts I brought them.
And a father, greyer, shrunken, sadly happy
To greet his wayward daughter, thinking the long
Enchantment over, that I would be home forever.
Weeks spilled into the bowl of months,
And the world wrapped round me in a whirl of doing.

It wasn't till the mirror spoke one twilight,
When the eaves dripped ominous drizzling rain.
Within its compass was a terrible sight:
Only a little breath stirred his broad chest,
His lustrous eyes were dim and narrowing with pain,
He scarcely had the power to call my name.
I had forgotten him, was his silent last reproach.

## BEAUTY AND THE BEAST

Rain-drenched through a wild night's riding,
I flew to his shuddering side and wept my love.
'Too late and parted,' came the chorus of a distant song,
But I laid my lips over the snarl of his twisted mouth,
Chafing the talloned paws with my human fingers.
The shimmer that lit upon him I thought death
And broke a death-keen from my grief-clenched throat.

The glimmer changed him: at my disenchanting kiss,
The bivalve horns dropped from him, claws retracted,
His bison bulk diminished and his mouth grew straight,
More kissable than before. From his stretched scalp
Black curls rioted over his handsome ugly face.
Only the trusting eyes were still his, and the soul
That shone out of him into my heart.

Of course, we were married: that was the story
That followed the happily-ever-afterness.
But now we have breakfast, lunch and tea together,
Not just dinner; and after dinner; we explore
The outer constellations of love,
Though the nights are never long enough
To savour the long disenchantment of that kiss.

# VERSES TO JOHN

### i
### AN UNEQUAL MUSIC

In the amazement of your arms,
I have only the stammer of unequal music:
Dreams of a symphony,
And in my mouth
Only the one-stringed fiddle of my love.

### ii
### PRAISING EAGLES

Finding power on the banks of want,
You disprove the rule
That on the verge of extinction
Species rarely flourish.
As my heart's hope droops wing,
Your new-found faculty
Flies out of an ancient place:
Within the eyrie shines a clutch of eggs.

## VERSES TO JOHN

### iii
### THE MENDING

Your pain has cracked stone:
Mountains are fissured with the rubble of your heart.
But I have made harbours
That it may slide safely
Into the kindness of the green sea.
By stealth of night it shall be mended,
Till only by vein's lesion shall
You know it was ever shattered.
Each wave's curl shall roll you;
You shall be whorled in the shaping ocean;
By wind and water, you will be made whole.

### iv
### A HARD WOMAN?

Life has grained me granite
Where ravens haunt their kill;
Even the sun shines steely on my slopes.

But know I am so soft,
You could put your finger through me.
I am a sanctuary of secret chalk,
Wanting only a votary to tend and pray.

Those who love me know the grain
Running like silk through my stone side:
A thread of kindnesses cleaves me to the web.

VERSES TO JOHN

## I WILL BE YOUR BONNY
*for John*

I will come with you and be your bride,
Though the way be long and roads be narrow.
I will keep my faith though gossips chide.
I will come with you and be your bonny.

I will walk with you wher'ere you go,
I will walk with you through rain or weather.
When the blackbird sings, when snowflakes fall,
I will keep you close wher'ere we wander

I will take the road with you beside,
Though the sun go down, or stars diminish.
I hold your hand in deepest dark,
I will dream the way and be your bonny.

# WITHIN KABALISTIC MEMORY

> 'When a soul is sent down from heaven,
> it is a combined male and female soul.
> The male part enters the male child
> and the female part enters the female.
> If they are worthy, God causes them
> to re-unite in marriage. This is true mating.'
> —*The Zohar*

God's likenesses spill from the fountain of your mind,
Drops that bless the face, making it shine:
Running gematria, permutating like holy algebra,
Across the limits where no words can travel.
Make dwelling for me too, you who dwell with letters,
In the alphabetic temple of memory, clothed with the covenant,
That I may have belonging and true name!

I long to smell lemons, to snuff the nutmeg through its grater,
To lift the warm *challa* from its white cloth,
To rest within fragrant sabbaths that stretch on and on.
The licence of your love permits me

## WITHIN KABALISTIC MEMORY

To wind phylacteries about my arm
And wear the seal of angels on my brow;
Your gracious loving is the *tallis* enfolding my heart.

When I am oned with you, when number ceases to matter,
Only the peacock ocean shall proclaim the glory.
Magic shall fly on magpie wings, steal from the very nest
The sapphire that bestows true sight of God:
That gem that is a portionless book, a power
Hovering on the brink, celestial and conspiring,
Read only on the wind by those who find their *beresheit*. (beloved other)

When we are yoked in one egg,
When stars rim the fragile shell of heaven,
It shall be eternal meat, the table where we dine
    on one another.
Words shall be bread, love become wine.
And the holy scrolls, wound back to the beginning,
Shall melt back peacefully into an ocean
Bluer than sapphire, more precious than flame.

I am become a tunnel where memory echoes
And all your appearances since Adam are the breath of Eden.
Through seven days the cantillation of your praise
Has sung the universal measure, love and all existences.
A reed so fragile, swelled by the calling of your mouth,
I am a music through the wisdom tree, singing in its branches:
'I am the Sabbath Queen and you my Crown.'

# MYTHS

# MYTH LAND

Don't stop me! I am going
Into the myth-land where Alice went
Where cards and chessmen
Are my companions.
And where the fall of cards discloses:
There I am queen of all the roses.
Trumps and triumphs have their day,
But here is my own land of play.

# THE TIME OF MAGIC

It was a time when magic lived in trees
And fairies cavorted nightly
At the bottom of my garden
Where densely planted shrubbery
Gave them mythic cover,
Though they never played with me.

And from the old encyclopedia
I drew stories of the myths that matter:
Pegasus, Perseus and the Gorgon head,
The tale of the tree and Osiris'
Resurrection; and I, the lone heroine,
In search of a myth of my own.

I found it on the downland chalk,
Under the shade of long-felled trees,
Where I was an Artemis in my running,
Spear poised ready for attack,
A severe and Spartan girl
Dedicated to the mythic chase.

And in the play-ground I told tales
Of the pigs that run before dawn,
The blue woman who brings vengeance,
The red girl who gifts sweetness.
And I made those orphaned of the story
Into hero-bands who roamed the glen with me.

Those fearless days are never done.
There is no night without a star.
Brave-deeds bring their own reward.
Courage to sacrifice brings strength.
And all these truths I do believe
Who walks still the mythic road.

# WHERE THREE CRANES FLY AT DAWN

He has gone into the turning house,
Where three cranes fly at dawn.
By ancestral causeway of the troytown's spin,
He takes flight,
Leaving his letters on the dancing wind.

King of the Summer Country,
He takes flight.
Soul-passager of the sevenfold turn,
Over the sea-bull's back,
Where three cranes fly at dawn.

Ancestrally, the dancers take to light,
Where three cranes fly at dawn.
By vast and sea-beguiling strand,
He takes flight:
His seaweed garland left within my hand.

# WHEN ANCIENT STARLIGHT FALLS TO EARTH

The sacred king, his holy duty done,
He takes flight.
Leaving his quiet Helen here to mourn,
Queen of the last Troy under sun,
Where three cranes fly at dawn.

# Homeward the Heroes

Only the heroes venture to this shore
Who dared sea-monsters and the raging doubt
That strength alone was unacceptable;
Who sought out hardships tougher than the rest,
Sailing that one sea further to the world's edge
To vastation of familiar comforts.

Now, at the landfall, to be brought to bed
Each with the gifting maiden of his heart,
Safe in the deep enchantment of her arms.
Confederate with the cauldron, long-brewed
To boiling by the ninefold breath,
Each drinks a draught of lengthening life,
Each forks the joint of meat he best desires.

All have a hero's portion without stint,
Wrapped in a mystery that finds no flaw,
Until the unfixed date which soon shall dawn
When heroes wake remembering they are men.
Then to the vessel shall they stumbling stretch,

To trim the tackle, skimming the keel of sea-wrack,
Seized with the discontent that is mortality.
Craving their wives' rough admonitions,
The untidy sprawl of children round their feet.

None to his fellow dares to voice his dream
Yet all are longing for returning tides,
Singing the way to homewards in their hearts.
Replete with knowledge that they are not gods:
Mere mariners begotten between sheets who sought
Immortal singing and unending fame.
To the forgiving surge they set their course again.

But can there be a true returning
For those who have dreamed within the heart of dream,
Whose blood has been infused within the cauldron,
Whose deeds shine diademed on each horizon?
Star-shut, bird-shout, on a far-shored dawning,
Finds familiar inlets and remembered harbour.
Earth grips each foot as showers thankful fall,
Heroic feats diminish to daily toils,
The deeds of gods to ploughmen's labour turned.

Still by the firelight, in the embered gleads,
The island lives enchanted. Each long-recounted
Deed is recollected with a grimaced smile
That to the gathered children paints a time
Of torments undergone, and speaks to young men
Of a tender maiden's glancing touch.
While wives wisely write-off the years
Of absence and a barren bed, glad to embrace
A body seamed by scars in far-off wars
And know herself a goddess still adored.

# THE MYTH IS YET LIVING
## A SONG FOR JOHN

It's the truth that I tell you:
The myth is yet living.
By the bright fingered dawning and the twilight so true.
May your story awaken!
To its own house be taken,
That you may arise with the heroes of old.

I am taking the books down
And coaxing the stories
From covers whose closure has kept out the dream.
And I've smoothed out the paper
And laid your pen ready
That when you return you can write the next scene.

From the rack of despair
Let your limbs be unfolded
And dance the glad round of the seasons again.
May your thoughts be unpinned
From sad campaign's defeating
And the savour and flavour embrace you again.

# WHEN ANCIENT STARLIGHT FALLS TO EARTH

There are years that lie wasted,
Sweet poems untasted,
There are memories that whirl like the wind-haunted leaf.
But the fields are ploughed ready
And the earth's still believing
The seeds of your life shall raise up a gold sheaf.

From your long empty wanderings
In dry desert places,
Come sit by the curve of the wide ocean's shore.
And play in the tide
Of my fathomless loving
And be one with me always in peace, love or war.

It's the truth that I'm telling:
The myth is yet living,
By each dream and footfall, each touch of the hand.
And the vision still flames
In the bright heart of darkness,
But the heroes and stories all bear our own names.

# MINOTAUR

In earth of earth,
The double aulos sounds,
In echo of the embryonic beast,
And of his sleep they sing:

'Rumoured are his strange epiphanies,
The deep earth-bull and chorus-man:
Minótauros, Asterion.'

The ever-double note
Has troubled us,
Who know his dual nature in our blood.

They sing:
'Behold the dead and living one,
His flowering blood out-spilt,
The riven unity, our doused spark:
Bright Dionysus.'

## WHEN ANCIENT STARLIGHT FALLS TO EARTH

There is running-dance and earth shake
In the song.
The lowing pipes stretch out their necks
And weep.
Their breath a weary soughing
In the reed:
'He is undone, dismemberéd.
Our plains are bare
Where once he stamped.
Where once the mares answered
His speed,
They moan and tremble for his covering.'

'Where have we trespassed
That his weight be gone?'

The sly and double answer echoes still:
'He is not dead.
Beyond the stars his birth,
His sleep, beneath the hill.'

# ESSENTIAL MYTHOLOGIES

Starved of the deep mythologies,
We drown in daylight, robbed of night;
Where markless mediocrities
Bind fast the eyes with blinding light.

We keep not faith; the stories seep
Under horizons of belief,
Till crouching trollwise, out they crawl,
Shrunken shadows without any teeth.

Breach-born abortions strut the screen,
Spreading their blood-starved emblems out
In semblance of the rich-hued myths
That brightened the soul and conquered doubt.

Reality one-sided runs:
Filleted fragment without a bone,
A bleached escarpment bare of rock,
Where silent screamings shriek alone.

## WHEN ANCIENT STARLIGHT FALLS TO EARTH

Before the proud technocracies
Had sucked the stream of vision dry
And cast dust's pall upon the tale,
Mocking the myth with idiot's bray,

The saving story spread its wings
From sea to sea, shining its sun:
Glad telling told by many tongues,
A song that shone when we began.

Lest what is timeless go unmarked,
I lend my ever-willing pen
To dip within the visioning well
That wisdom's salmon spawn again.

Dive to the deep beloved dark
That raises up the living verse,
To bring the stories brightwise up,
To ransom from the depthless curse

All who acclaim the naked lie
That trustless is the womb of dark.
May they the breast-myth sup once more,
Suckling the muse-milk from its spark!

# A GREEN KILLING

We kill you
       but the green pours from your mouth
              faster than scythe can slice.

Green Jack
       merry dancer of the trees
              we dream of you within the forest maze.
Play at echo
       though you call the tune
              a game of catch and can through bounteous days.

We kill you
       yet the green comes pouring through
              despite the sharpening of the reaping hook.

Hay-making
       triumphantly piling up
              magnificently forking spikes of sweet grasses.

## WHEN ANCIENT STARLIGHT FALLS TO EARTH

Intoxication of seed-heads
> riotously glorying in sunshine
>> spreading the green-seed far on every side.

We kill you
> yet the green comes tumbling down
>> straight from the regions of the burnished sun.


Viriditas
> his kingly cloak puts on
>> peers through the arbour of the nascent green.

His chap-Jack cheeks
> pout with the winds' bright breath
>> blazoning summer while the lark shrills on.

'I green you
> though you cut me down
>> wait till winter when I come in high renown.'

The pollard trees
> their rasta locks unfurl
>> after the barber axe has trimmed their crowns.

The wych-elms lean together and conspire
> plotting new treacheries of lustier growth
>> pretending piety along the churchyard path.

We kill you
> and the green day halts its song
>> the woods are dying and cannot live long.

# A GREEN KILLING

Year-stop
    frost-fronds leaf the windowpane
        green withers to a dwindling brown.

Now come ivy-twine
    holly-curl yew-bite cedar-smite
        axe-grip your hunger in the hollow hall.

'I fed you
    when the summer days were long
        now feed me while I wield the winter song.'

Green King
    you are lord of larders all
        have mercy on each stricken breath we draw.

Remember us
    who played within your wood
        our shining man, our master, and our good!

'I greened you
    yet you cut me down
        now comes the reckoning to adorn my crown.'

# WRITTEN IN GOLD

Whatever you do when you die,
Hold fast to memory.
When you stand in Hades' house you'll find
To the right, under a white cypress,
A well where dead souls quench their thirst.
Do not go near it, Lethe's well!
Beyond it find the Spring of Memory,
Cool water flowing clean.
The guardians will ask,
'What do you seek from the shades of Hades' house?'

Answer quickly, say at once,
'I am a child of earth and starry heaven,
I am dry with thirst and dying,
But give me quick the cool waters
From the Spring of Memory.'
And they will pity you,
By the will of Queen Persephone,
And give you water from Mnemosyne's spring.

## WRITTEN IN GOLD

Then will you go on the Sacred Way,
In company with other initiates,
And with the inspired ones upon their way.
On your breast I lay these words,
Written in gold, that you will never die.

# Arthur Wakens Everywhere

In the child who plays alone,
In the elder's faltering step,
In the lovers' secret moan,
Arthur wakens everywhere.

In the grove condemned by axe,
In the hill that's bulldozed flat,
In the hedgerow chain-sawed down,
Arthur wakens everywhere.

In the hand that stays the axe,
In the mind that fights despair,
In the step that walks the track,
Arthur wakens everywhere.

In the wandering tribes reborn,
In the chill of workless homes,
In the office blocks forlorn,
Arthur wakens everywhere.

# ARTHUR WAKENS EVERYWHERE

In the coastal path's embrace,
In the inland rivers fair,
In the hope of every face,
Arthur wakens everywhere.

In the deep ancestral tomb,
In the spiral vision's track,
In the opening of the womb,
Arthur wakens everywhere.

In the blackbird's twilight song,
In the owl's midnight cry,
In the dawn larks' soaring throng,
Arthur wakens everywhere.

Out of darkness, out of sleep,
Out of despite and despair,
Out of songs and stories deep,
Arthur comes to banish care.

Now the sleepers cease their rest,
Now the sacred circle turns,
*Now and here,* in every breast,
Arthur's guardian image burns.
Join the circle and the singing,
Cast away doubt and despair,
Ancestor and children bringing,
Arthur wakens everywhere.

# SURVIVORS OF CAMLANN
## AD 542

### SANDDE ANGEL-FACE

To be always beautiful is a curse, he'd always thought.
To be framed as maiden, with clustering lashes
and a fair, straight body that turned heads,
was beneath the dignity of a warrior.
He fought for his place in the line, fended off
the smiles and favours bestowed so freely,
stood in the long lines with shield and sword,
a man among men. And he'd not shuddered
at the first clash of shields, nor groaned as spear-points
thrust at his shapely sides. With a man's courage
and an angel's face he'd grimaced at the enemy,
but none would engage with him. They saw
Baldur, blessed of Wodin; they saw Mabon,
only lamented son of the Mother, Modron
of the calamitous, orphaning blows; they saw
Christ striding over death with glory wings
and turned their points from him,

not to be exiled from hope of Valhalla,
nor apple-bright Avalon, nor angelled paradise.

Nor would any man break swords with him.
And so it was that he saw the severing blow
of Medrawt's spear, saw the emperor stoop
over the heart-seeking blade, saw the gush
of his dear-won death spasm... and would have
given every ounce of beauty to have been
the vengeance of Britain's blade, when Arthur's
sword struck upwards in his black son's gut
and all was done. Even afterwards, that anguish
writ upon his face, Sandde's smile still shone
so that men asked what good news he carried
when they met upon unpeopled roads.
And his angel's voice answered, bitter as bile,
that at Camlann, Arthur fell and Britain died;
but questioners went onwards and told tales
that an angel spoke from Camlann's field
of Avalonian enchantment and release,
with high hope in their hearts for evermore,
and felt them blessed to have encountered him.
With god-cursed lamentation, Sandde
hid his face and gladdened no woman's heart
his whole life long.

---

## MORFRAN AP TEGID

On seeing him laid in her arms, his mother had resolved
to make him a cauldron of knowledge, so that there might
be some mitigation for the features he'd been birthed with.
But that draught was sunk by some minion set to mend the fire

and Morfran had escaped with only his ugliness for company.
Commanded to the forefront of battle, he stepped up
to the lime-shield wall and smiled his demon's smile.
And where he gazed, gaps opened, in the shrinking lines.
Men ran from the pursuit of Fenrir wolf, or from
Gwyn's wild-hunt ride, or from the ravening tusks of
Twrch Trwyth's mad career. Horses reared up and fled.
On that dark field, Morfran left only the dead.

## ST CYNFELYN

Reluctantly into battle, he rode on a borrowed horse,
the son of chiefs and warriors, with no battle-leader's lust
to ferment his prayers. From the speed of his horse
he made good his escape and lived to tell of it.
But his pride smarted, and he told tales of the conflict
that were praise-reflecting on his undone deeds,
and—because there were few to rebuke him
—got away with it.

## ST CEDWYN

One good man goes from the world
as breath is drawn each second.
God knows he prayed for the emperor, knowing
from the small hour's confession, a soul whose care
was for the little folk of Britain as much as for the great.
Cedwyn was spared from the world's blessing, from every
needful one who ever found God's bounty at his hands;
his way through the field was in pity, and so he was ransomed

out of the wreck, his every merciful step lined with candles
put up by the small folk, their prayers as arrows against
the enemy. And he walked through the fray
as men stroll through meadows, breathing blessing
on each fair head.

---

## ST PEDROC

Reluctantly a saint, he'd always been a spear-bearer;
his place in the lines of men, not up a hillside
with acolytes and bell-ringers. By spearmanship
he was saved, and by ancient and unchristian skills
learned long in battalions and practice yards.
His faith was a spear bright as Lleu's long arm,
daintily darting between wren's bands of
Saxon-swelled Britons of Medrawt, that puny wren
who'd wrought winter in Caerleon's round.
Spear-men might cage that miscreant whelp
of the Great Bear, who tried usurping
the sun-blessed reign of Emperor Arthur!
So he pulled a spear out of the rack
and he'd rode down, despite protesting clerics,
into the fast-packed multitudes below.
But the wren had already pierced the
golden bear and the dragon drooped
over the throng in a hushed wind.
And Petroc rode westwards, lamenting
that chrism had conquered the weapon-grease
of his convert's heart.

# DERFEL THE STRONG

None could withstand the shock of his arm
which, strong as lightening-shot oak,
struck Jovian blows uncaringly from side to side.
Imperishable strokes bore him from the field,
only because there were no more enemies left.
And if afterwards his dull-headed gloom was
unremittingly dark, there were none to challenge
why his deep-veined arm hadn't shielded the
emperor from the death-entering blow.
His term of life was long extended, as if vengeance
could be wrought upon the years in recompense.
And at his death, his stoic and unspeaking gloom
had fuelled talk of sainthood; because of his hermit
solitude, men took his silence for prayerful retreat.
They carved an image from Brythonic oak-bogs
and with a pagan splendour prayed loudly
to the Strong Derfel and his long protection.
And so he was remembered till butcher Cromwell
wrought a reformation; in Smithfield fires,
they say the long-enduring wood of that saint
cast cold shadow rather than heat
and that five strong oaks were felled
to burn away the ancient blackness of that image.

## GENEID THE TALL

First to engage and last to leave. His speed
led men to the first shield-shock and he rode through
and back, determined to make his mark. But he
stood tall in the saddle and, save for some wounds
on his thigh, he turned like wind through churned-up barley.
Like a standard, his helmet shone with westering sun,
his keen horse wheeling in the battling throng
with piercing neigh, and none stood against them,
Until Arthur fell.

He fought the fight beyond Camlann
Till the years grew thick upon him
Like the chains of freedom once remembered.
And when kingdom after kingdom went down to the dark,
Into exile he went, stooped but a little by the years.

And yet he sat for centuries in a cave,
    contemplating the distancing seas.
And if he yearned for company,
    none could tell it, for none beheld him.
That there existed freedom this rare
    was only the eagles' knowledge.
The eyrie's isolation for him
    was not prison but nest
Where the incubation of work
    might be accomplished alchemically.
Even till his dried bones blew,
    dislodged by the winds of centuries,
    there the seat of freedom remained.
And his bone-dust fell like snow
    on the soiled trammels of imprisoned hearts.

# DIVINITIES & SPIRITS

# DAIMONIC SEQUENCE
## FOUR POEMS FOR MY MASTER-SPIRIT

i
*Totemic Entry*

There was no means of knowing,
Since he entered as a man,
How the room was filled with beasts—
Hocked, horned, feathered—
His breath like seraphims',
Gorgeously apparelled in glory.

Since his entering in,
There is no telling
This world from the other.
His teeming shapes turn,
—Hoof, paw, talon—
Since I entered into light,
The world is full of eyes,
As of eagles.

## ii
*The Days of Darkness*

My bright daimon dead,
And I despairing.
Quick-silvered spirit fled
And I preparing
His last memorial.

For he was Janus-headed,
Dream-herder
Of a thousand bedded
Sleeps. Murder
Of a matchless master.

He was my wholesome lord,
My making,
My bread, my board,
My own leave-taking,
And his end, my end.

This last beginning dark
Without fire.
These words a lightless mark,
A leaden gyre—
A life guttering out.

## DAIMONIC SEQUENCE

iii

*Spirit Harper*

He dies not, but is changed—
I saw him in the prophet's chorus,
Singing, and my heart was glad.
Virgil, Dunbar, Abelard—
Master-makers, chorusing.

For you have harped and mastered me;
Strung me unprotesting to your mode.
I have died in your music, been rewoven
On the lyre of the world. Oh Master!
Make me virgin and restore the light!

iv

*Dawn Song*

Dawn is fled.
On the steps of the walled garden
They sing your *alba*.
On the stepped fretwork,
Angelic notes ascending.

Notes spill from the oud
As the fountain gathers.
On the steps of the walled garden,
Where they come to draw water,
Women sing your *alba*
And sigh for envy.

# WHEN ANCIENT STARLIGHT FALLS TO EARTH

You taught Areopagite and Abelard
Through the lute's discourse,
And—more subtle teaching—
Attic Eros, Ovidian Amor.

But to no earthly mistress
Are your musics made.
Nine brightnesses with nine lanterns
Light your way over the grey seas.

# THE OLD WOMAN OF BEARE

i
*Christian*

An unnatural thing: hurrying east of west.
The yeast of me scurrying widdershins.

All things speed deosil: caught each wing,
Beached each fin: fraught with sin.

Ploughs point north—seed toil in stars.
Uncoiled, each ragged weed dies haggard.

My grianan's south, where suns uncover
A nun's despair—youth's disrepair.

I'll make no journey east! Bright my hopes once:
This sky lends distance to my sight, my self-reproach.

I'll coax the western wind, scull his tides on each approach
To my islanded west and a homely coast.

## ii
*Pagan*

I who am Anu, Buí and Brighid
Sit anchored to a fireside.
Despite the cleric's ire,
I am one who sinned well.

The four winds in my bag:
Each tower they'll topple down to hell.
Unleashed, my curses fluently
Will quell each cloistered hag.

And saints now chaste and virgin
I'll corrupt; each pilgrim sell
His relics to embrace a nun.
The culdee slakes his fast on sturgeon.

All kinds of sexual sport and harmless fun
I will let loose. No innocents
May plead exemption: at every airt
I'll make them seem degenerates.

They'll lip no creed. In every part
The quiet clip of thigh and heart—
The *paters* and the *aves* die
In homage to my faithful craft.

# SOVEREIGNTY'S CHALLENGE

I am the rage, I am the wildness
—I also am the queen's quietness—
I am wildness, I am wilderness
—I also am her clipped enclosure.

I am the lightening in the darkness
—I also am the curtained dawn—
I am the violent earth's uprooting
—I also am the rocks reborn.

I am the wheeling flighting carrion
—I also am the gentle wren—
I am the toothed and darting weasel
—I am the white doe of the ben.

I am the molten rocks in motion
—I also am the patient stone—
I am the scouring streams of thaw-time
—I also am the gentle rain.

# WHEN ANCIENT STARLIGHT FALLS TO EARTH

Here is no shelter
—but my cloak is ready—
Here is no defence
—yet my shield is steady.

Lance but your winged shaft
against my heart—
my love, you shall be master
of my every airt.

# FEAST OF THE QUEEN OF SNOWS

Hasped in mist, the mountain locks its secret from the sea,
Her silent majesty evokes an ancient sovereignty:
Each notched escarpment, jagged breast, a craggy diadem;
Gouged from her rock, each mirrored loch a sky-reflecting gem.
And mantling every deep-thewed groin, the yellowing birch tree
    grows,
With rowan-crested sentinels to guard the Queen of Snows.
Her raven ministers haunt her glens, perch in the twisted pine,
While fish dispute each owed tribute, send up their bubbling sign.

Sun shields its spear, a druid brume slides down the echoing loch,
An ancient statecraft wreathed in mist makes parliament at her rock.
Here comes no man, no earth-bound ghost, but spirits of the land,
Assembled from the strataed hills to kiss her hallowed hand.
They rise, unheralded and strong, they keep their oath-bound tryst,
From tales untold, from bard and scald, they leap from rocky kist.
Acclaim with praise eternal days that die not nor are dimmed,
Delighting her with dreams fulfilled, with loyalties binding brimmed.

## FEAST OF THE QUEEN OF SNOWS

Night folds its sovereign cloak of dark about her shoulders strong,
The spiralling planets thread her hair with sparks of jeweled song.
The Merry Dancers throng night's hall, with throbbing rags of light,
Each keen to snatch her in their arms up to the dancing height.
With leaping arcs of rainbowed frost, they bow, then turn again,
The Queen of Snows, on upstretched toes, greets all her loyal men.
Long may she reign, her fastness stand, her stately line endure!
Stars catch the echo of their shout, drawn by her mystery's lure.

This autumn morning, quenched by cloud, she casts her glory down,
She dons apparal of the year, in brackens red and brown.
About her skirts, the heron stalks, the buzzard casts its shadow,
Dull are the jewels, and dour the slopes of the grey untitled widow.
Birch, oak and rowan fade and thin, while pine crowds green and close,
And none would guess, within their breast, what secret fire grows.
The mountain's mystery, ancient truth, lies locked and has no key,
Her secret safe within the spark that kindles liberty.

Realm of the ancient north, I claim my ancient lineal share,
Unmothered girl, both wise and fool, I beg a mother's care.
A daughter of this sacred land, from the uncaring south,
Your nurture and your wildness seeks, with parched and hungry mouth.
While royal rule its wheel still runs, I follow in its furrow,
Setting aside my happiness to heal the ancient sorrow.
Enduring Queen, with hope I come to kiss your royal hand,
With loyalty's oath and heart-struck truth, to love your sacred land.

# PRAYERS

# PRAYER OF THE BIRDS

All the prayers that were ever in my head
Clapped their wings like birds,
Away they fled.

And there was left only the unspoken prayer
Hanging in the falling rain
Like a spiral stairway leading everywhere.

A sudden entry into perpetual singing
Where words were coloured music,
Fragrant light,

Where all the world was bringing itself to a crest
That was ecstatic silence,
Dancing rest.

The branches of my brain became a tree
Whereon birds
Roosted trustfully,

A chantry-house perpetually calling
The twilight hours
Of every prayer.

In that enchanted hour there was only power,
Soundless, indivisible,
Shimmering under the wings of my heart

And I was part of all that had ever been
Or would ever be,
In the prayer that was praying me.

# I SHALL TAKE POETRY AS MY PRAYER

Dream and poetry, they are the augurs,
Freers at the doorjamb, blindfold at dawn,
Scanning the far and the near horizons
For signs of the mystery in fish and swan.

Keepers of the prescient twilight
Marking the ring where the fair-folk dance,
Hastening the hour of midnight's making,
Sun in the darkness illumining trance.

Prayer of the breath, inspire and fold me,
Prayer of my sleep, be vision-wise,
Prayer that entrances, sings and dances,
Keep me till dawning when I'll rise!

# Nomad's Prayer

Releasing the past, unknowing of the future
I inhabit this present place.
No God judges, rewards or punishes me.
I owe no-one my reward nor stain another with my judgement.
Joy rises with the dawn,
Abundance flows to my present need
When I abide in the gift of this moment.

Falling into the moment,
I cease to appease the past,
I disentangle the future.
When the road unreels each moment.
Fate is a turning spindle,
And destiny a fine thread
Running through my fingers.

When I live each moment,
I cleanse the garment of the past,
Arresting the future's stain.

# WHEN ANCIENT STARLIGHT FALLS TO EARTH

When I wear each naked moment,
I come richly caparisoned.
Pain and expectation shrink
As I walk the road with a song.

# BONE SONG

I was gorse on the track beaconing the way,
I was seal in the sea, braving the swell,
I was wind-cuffer mounting the bitter winds,
I was cloud billowing higher than Hoy.

I was the stillness of midwinter sun,
I was the gleaming in the causeway stone,
I was the narrow waist between two lochs.
I was chaff from the quern when oats were spun.

I was prey clutched in eagle's claws,
I was mist rainbowed over squall.
I was yellow flag over the black bog,
I was the fish between otter's paws.

All these have called to your dancing round,
In fire's glead, in star's seed, when you slept sound.
Before I am led to the ancestors' home,
Listen the song of my splintered bone.

# SPELL-SONG TO RESTORE THE EARTH

By our devoted prayer, by native birth,
We rock the land asleep within our dreams.
A tale un-seamed by darkness runs its rote;
By our glad living we restore the earth.

Worth every toil, apprenticed to the song,
(We rock the land asleep within our dreams)
Bringing back blessing from the furthest eaves
Of Western Isles, where falls no rain nor wrong.

Strong is the door that guards the island's life!
(A tale un-seamed by darkness runs its rote.)
The Blessed Head lies under for our peace;
He who unearths that Head shall raise up strife.

Life after life, regenerate to the last,
(By our glad living we restore the earth)
Each branching tribe its tributary singer lends,
Sharing the promise of ancestral past.

# SPELL-SONG TO RESTORE THE EARTH

Cast the bright seeds and care not where they lie:
(By our devoted prayer, by native birth,)
Songs seed in blood, within the fertile earth,
Dormant for ages, may they never die!

    By our glad singing we restore the earth;
    A tale sewn up with joy becomes our coat.
    We sing the world awake within our dreams
    By virtue of our prayer and native birth.

*Sanday, Orkney*

# PEOPLE

# COMPANIONS IN THE DARK
## FOR BRIAN KEENAN AND TURLOUGH O'CAROLAN

Hostage and harper were together in that prison:
An enduring friendship, taking no account of time.
Through pain's dull and brutalizing prism,
Protestant yoked to Catholic, for their crime.

On the febrile chords of memory you struck hands,
So that one shiver passed through each the same,
Though you lay in sundered times, different lands,
Yet you broached a meeting. So began the game

Of hide and seek, beyond the barriers of fear:
Strange companions, each huddled in the dark
Of his own blindness, with no harp nor writing gear.
Yet there was living brightness, an urgent spark

That leapt from heart to heart. A deal was struck:
'Brother, get me out of here, and I will do the like for you.
When I walk free—if fate will countersign my luck—
And I will speak to them of what you once held true.

For men need music, music of the mind,
To sheath their souls in woman's loving look,
To touch in every place the decent and the kind,
Bringing hope to those whom cruelty has shook.'

And, for his part, the harper was as good as his word,
Coming at unfrequented hours of night,
His story blown on echoes, urgent to be heard,
Gifting mind's denser image in the unseen light.

Your four years and a half imprisonment were done:
You walked, a free man, hollowed out of pain,
Into green and vibrant Ireland from dry Lebanon,
And the harper walked beside you in the rain.

Yet he, still prisoned in you, brought to mind
The debt of honour you had yet to pay.
And so, for friendship's sake, you paid in kind:
An equal story for each lightless, untold day.

Strings are not silent: nerve and note still chime
Their musics on the winds' free gale.
You are still brothers, on holiday from time,
Sharing the wisdom of the soul's true tale.

You said maybe there'd been space in you for him,
That, called or uncalled, he was a welcome traveller.
Despite your wondering why, now he's limb of your limb,
And only God can be your souls' unraveller.

# THE LANTERN BEARER
## IN MEMORY OF ROSEMARY SUTCLIFF, CBE
## 14 DECEMBER 1920–23 JULY 1992

In a quiet Candlemas garden,
Under the Arundel downs,
A partridge-plumaged woman
Sits in a lozenged gown.

She scribes her stories slowly
With a blunt old fountain pen,
Keeping faith with the history
Of forgotten women and men.

The ribboned page flows before her—
Celtic curved and Roman straight;
At the end of the journey, a welcome,
A bite and sup at the gate.

Bright sword to fight for freedom,
Round shield for fierce defence:
She scribes adventures slowly,
Tales simple and intense.

# THE LANTERN BEARER

Maimed heroes, quiet heroines,
She releases from the dark;
They bring the brand of brightness
From the ancient fire's spark.

Dear Britain is their burden,
Her coastlands' circled seas;
The manner of Her warfare,
The bringing of Her peace.

In native bothy and villa,
The song is just the same;
And the song the first ones chanted,
Is the one their descendants claim:

'Let the dark not overwhelm Her,
Let Her not fall unsung,
May Her dear remembered stories
Be quickened on every tongue.'

In the snow-drop carpeted garden,
The white doves circle and spin;
The woman writes no longer,
Her wooden foil to win.

Released now from the arena,
She walks the hillsides broad,
To share the crust of stranger,
To offer her own bright sword.

Unto the silent border,
Where the lost lone legions stand,
To welcome a new supporter
To patrol the dear-won land.

## THE LANTERN BEARER

These are the lantern-bearers
Who keep the disputed shore
Against all ruthless invaders
Who would trample the unwrit law.

Their courage kept clear the pathway,
Their hope stretched night to dawn,
They have maintained the true ways
For all free peoples born.

And now they lift their lanterns
To the one in the lozenged gown;
Who has been a lantern-bearer
Worthy of great renown.

The birds of Rhiannon call her
Beyond the curtained rain,
To the indwelling tribal fire,
To tell Britain's stories again.

# He Was Made Music
## In Memory of Dylan Thomas

He was made music in the lilting house
When green and gold he grew into a tree
And winds harped nightly on his strings
  Shaking the wastrel words
  That drink had not yet reeved
    Loose about the street.
  And because of these strange things
  I am commanded not to douse
      The living light
      But set as wings
  The praise songs of his leaves.

For he was green and burning from the start:
Promise-showering, fertile, verdant, lean,
Yet saturate with oil that waits the flame.
  Beneath the wind he cruised,
  Angelic demon fallen out of heaven.
    Bohemian King's Road lad,
Who never used one single word the same
    In all his craft or sullen art:

## HE WAS MADE MUSIC

> Metaphorical eclipse,
> Bewildering gleam,
> Verses with their own mysterious leaven.

Within the rattling tenement of his skin,
He lanced against the closure of the tomb.
Wrestling his double in a doubtful bout,
>   Confounding skeleton
>   With the living tree
>   Whose leaves he furled.
He his own semblance kissed, then promptly smote,
Whirled away rib-fellow with a grieving grin,
>   Off-cast the yoke-mate
>   Of his albumen
Back to the egg-shell darkness of womb's sea.

Child of the singing valleys, he grew down:
A raging foetus beating on the bone,
With words that sang like wires to his tune.
>   An angry, unlapped cupid,
>   Made for love,
>   Cheated of Venusberg.
Who turned the pick-lock of his heart's betrayal?
>   In the embraces of the harlot town,
>   He rode the death-weir
>   With a salmon's moan,
Seeking the womb-cot as his mother's dove.

But when October cocked his birthday clock,
Fettled his feathers with alchemical dew,
Cast the ungentle fetters of his exile off.
>   Chalybeate waters
>   Through dry valleys ran
>   Their exulting song.
He, the beloved of heaven, was summoned aloft

## HE WAS MADE MUSIC

Up to the riding nest to rock
Safe in the vessel,
Mercurially-
imbued,
Embraced by god-like gladness: a transfigured man.

He is made sheriff of the ancient trees,
Those that in Eden grew, before the flood.
From the dissenting chapel of his strife,
He druids back the grove
To potent flame,
Kindling the wicks of words.
Since he grew out of patience with his life,
He wooed each passing breeze
Till it sang through
His bone of blood
A gale, and blew away all but his poet's fame.

# TO HER SECRET BOWER
## A SONNET ON THE DEATH OF QUEEN ELIZABETH II ON 8TH SEPTEMBER 2022

Hearts are hollow at this empty hour,
Unready for the suddenness of flight.
Despite the anxious bulletins, our flower
Has hastened on before us into light.
*Noblesse oblige*, but *Honi Soit Qui Mal
Y Pense*. Oh, sirs, speak soft!
And do not prate of how unmonarchist
You are. Her majesty she has put off.

Unfailingly, the mother of us all,
Leans back into her secret hidden realm,
Deeper down within the great ancestral hall,
Recalled by those in hood and ancient helm.
And while the lion hurries with her unspent dower,
The unicorn kneels quiet in her bower.

# PLACES & JOURNEYS

# FAREWELL, YOU BRIGHT DANCERS

They pass, the bright dancers, down the long path of blood,
Leaving an empty story and a kicked-off shoe on the sod.
There's only a drift of music through the daily market's cry
And a long regret that impeaches the innocent Lenten sky.

Each of the dancing partners who swung me in their sway
Have passed like smoke from a hearthfire on a burning summer's day.
The passionate feet that bore me now dance to a different tune,
The love that was bright between us, turns dark as the changing moon.

I search for the shards of story upon a jagged shore,
As Isis in her mourning sought for the scattered lore.
Only the plaintive curlew its solitary fluting makes
As over the barren hillside an empty morning breaks.

The hollow daylight departing, I lift my pleading eyes,
And out of the gentle darkness, see destiny's star arise.
Down its shimmering pathway, the ancient promises ride,
A hope that the dancing had blinded, a sure and certain guide.

## WHEN ANCIENT STARLIGHT FALLS TO EARTH

A melody pure and perfect, a song from the heart of time,
Reverberates the darkness, making the dead boughs chime.
Fruits set on the fruitless branches as stars come tumbling out,
An untold story dances on the shivering shores of doubt.

# BEYOND THE NINTH WAVE

Before I journey to the many-coloured land,

I check supplies:
> marmite, herb tea, travel scrabble,
> (for you never know how boring eternity might be!)
> assorted books—some novels overdue a reading,
> some sustaining poetry, rich as cheese,
> and music—a harp to play upon,
> a tarot pack to divine how the ordinary world wags.

And because it is an island and rugged:
> an alpen-stock for climbing and a water-proof,
> sun-oil in case it shines and midge repellent
> (always necessary in August at twilight and wind-fall,)
> most optimistically, a swim-suit and sarong.

To keep in touch with the outside world:
> a strip of address labels to deserving friends
> who shall be written to briefly and poetically,
> but no mobile phone to invite the worry devils

## BEYOND THE NINTH WAVE

    to my silent island.

And, to propitiate the natives, who are wee and free
    (though not in our sense at all tolerant)
    a covering shawl, a long-sleeved dress
    some flat shoes and a Gaelic tutor
    (so that I may call greeting and condone the weather.)

My case is packed for earthly paradise
    (it shall return heavier though, especially
    once the shells and stones from beach and hill
    have sweet-talked their way into it.)
But my heart will be lighter for my sojourn
Beyond the ninth wave.

# BHALASAIGH SUNSET

Eight rushing streams shoot under the bridge,
Between Bhalasaigh and Tobson.
Otter spraint on the lochan's brink
Where freshwater cedes to salt.
At tide's break, the workmen halt
To play pooh-sticks under the slender arch,
Their digger lurching sideways.

The road-wideners make a turning place
For the ambulance. The man on crutches
Over the lochan has his path smoothed
For a wheelchair: the weaver and his wife
Have a place to roll their tweed in.
The peat-brown weed seethes in the tide-break,
Cauldrons of spate-water tumble with fish.

The nightly walk to Bosta is full of beaches:
Gull-ribs, sheep vertebrae, ruminant's teeth;
Shoaled in the kelp-wrack with burst floats,
Rubber gutting gloves, tangled blue netting.

# BHALASAIGH SUNSET

Below the plastic line, Lewisian gneiss
In a sweet-shop sprawl for beach-combing,
Provident fish-crates for retrieving.

Salt-soaked timber, blue-spiked supplements
To flame the peat in winter blazes.
As the seal-heads turn for their island,
The sun flames briefly and is spelled by cloud;
Our west Atlantic haunts a gold-rose distance.
The moon comes up to greet the stars;
Dusk renders the cuneiformed rocklets dumb.

My singing fire duets the cello wind:
I take my last dram and wind up the clock.
Coming to sleep and closure in one hour.
Peace-bright, the night comes rushing in:
Dreams flow tidal through my warm bedroom.
I am sand sifting on the sea-shore,
Shell-dust, remnant of a prouder rock.

*Isle of Lewis*

# SEA-MASTER
## FOR MANANNÁN MAC LIR

Who sea-gifted this shapely wood?—
His laugh-lines seam the beach.
His worship does not die:
Bride's bird does him due devotion.

None dare turn their back on him:
Only the sea-mew of the storm
Makes a long cast over the murk of squall,
And the ringed plovers who scurry from his wash
Like maiden ladies with soaked petticoats.

He's no respecter of the shore;
He transmogrifies, comes sea-booted in
Like any mariner, bent on beer and women.

By his watched margins I've danced, dared him
Visit me by night, sea-wanderer, so that, dawnwards,
I'll have to brush the sand from out my bed.

*Bay of Skail, Orkney*

# BOSHAM SEQUENCE

### i
### A QUIETING

Into the embracing quiet enter in,
Push back the heavy door;
The ways between lie delicate and dim.

Other visitants came here before,
Eager, penitent, beseeching grace:
Their dust still swirls serene and sure.

As introit sounds, lift up your face:
A company of the heavenly knighthood sings,
Hallowing this quiet place.

To all unquiet souls, their blessing brings
Deep housel, a belonging care,
The quench of all distressing things.

## BOSHAM SEQUENCE

Enter the embracing quiet, if you dare.
Bright in the darkness be you ever seen
In form of the heavenly vesture that you wear

Imbued with quiet, quit the leaden pall.
A holy life shall clothe you, innocent,
And bring you to the welcome of this call.

---

### ii
### HAROLD EMBARKS FROM BOSHAM

Slack tide by habourside,
The barques lie beached and still.
In six more hours they will embark
Over the Frankish main to Normandy.

Who knew the wrack-slimed stones
Hinted at infamy? The gospels hidden?
An oath that swore away the realm?
Now are we bidden to hold firm
Anchored in loyalty as the swell crests.

Full moon and flood tide high deeds favour.
Over the oar-rests, halt awhile, head turned:
We shall not see this homely harbour more.

---

## BOSHAM SEQUENCE

### iii
### CANUTE'S DAUGHTER

When wood violets bloom again
It will have been three sad years
Since our maiden left us,
Tripped and tumbled into the mill-race,
And none to mark her,
Till the oast-man's son
Saw where her footsteps slipped and raised the cry.
Dear fore-farer, whom we laid in earth,
Small Iphigenia of souls' embarkation.

When asphodels nod in the hedgerows
We'll remember her, tell how her
Danish father commanded the wave turn—
That never man called back—
As, sweet to salt, she floated down,
And his tears then, stark on the shore,
When she from wave was lifted.
All sleep in God, kept fast in howe
Till we be raised by angel's call.

When the Lenten lily palls,
Wise ones say we all shall be lifted.
Will our little maid, so venturesome,
Arise, hands stretched up, as they depone?
Or shall we see a shining company of folk
Made over in their first array,
Blithe and blessed on Easter morn?
And bubbling laughter in the brook,
Turn again, as on the day that she was born?

## BOSHAM SEQUENCE

### iv
### SEA WAYS

Sea ways sundered by the tide
The under-pull of full moon's clinch
Hauled away at harbourside.

Gravel sucked back by the ebb
Wave-spill lays its sandy bed
Spreads its pattern as night's web.

Chart-lines erased, lost voyages track
By dreams paid out on memory's seam,
A feint of journeys at wind's back.

The star-cup tilts, its weavings slide
To mornings fair and dawnings dim.
Our keels by night's unclasping glide.

A brimming sea the harbour fills
Pennants flutter on the breeze,
Farewell to secret, distant hills.

# VISIONS

# SEA LANTERNS

At the margin of the sea as I walked by
There came an old woman from the wave
Who swam into my hand, black as ebony.

From her wrinked navel she drew out
Three gifts for me: the sun, the moon,
And a shoal of stars with a glad shout.

And I, not fathoming her sublime reason,
Questioned the wisdom of her nakedness
And the glimmering treasures of that season.

It was the changing hour, when the broad skies
Stream with festal ribbonings of cloud,
When the fast tide neither flows nor flies.

'This day, I've gathered lights for your way,
Lanterns of brightness for the growing dark,
That you be safe-kept this night,' I heard her say.

And knew she meant by 'that day,' an aeon's wing,
Glancing the storm of fleeting centuries,
All to comfort a grand-child lost and lingering.

The moment trembled and turned: she was out of my hand,
A melting obsidian snow pearling to distance.
There was only the shivering dark and a lonely land.

And I clutched at the sands where her gifts had rolled:
Only a fleck of micaed gold, a cusped opalescence
Of shell and a limpet's ring that the sea had holed.

But I clutched them all the long way home:
For a promise of light is a gleam in the dark,
And hope is a spark when it leaps from the foam.

Though the long darkness mantle me in folds
Like the peat-bog's blanket these many miles,
Yet her ancestral guardianship still holds.

Old One, lost to the urn-ashed aeons, hark!
The song of your gifts still sings in the stream of blood;
I steer by your gleads in the sundering dark.

# IN PRAISE OF DARKNESS
## FOR THETIS BLACKER, SHAMANKA OF THE BATIK

The coils of the interwining
Clasp fast the egg-shell earth.
Yet what shall hatch in the darkness
But the golden bird of birth?

The bird that bears the brightness
Now opens wide its beak:
It flies to the tree of dawning,
Discoursing of the deep.

'Bright, it is bright in the darkness,
Though not to the eyes of the world.
Who clutches the pelt of darkness
Lays hand on the flame unfurled.'

Ah, bird in the branches singing,
We need your healing note.
Make bright the knowing darkness,
That it sing in every throat.

# IN DAZZLING DARKNESS
## FOR THE ANCIENT GAELIC POETS
## WHO COMPOSED IN DARKNESS

Like the salmon now, he sleeps in the dim weed
Of metaphor, waiting for a sudden phosphorescence
To lead him to the bright, bestowing spring
Where he was born, to spawn from heart's need
A tale untold, uttered only in the dark,
Spun by every seeker of life's spark.

Only the young discover the narrow way through the rock;
The upstream struggle to be free brings them straight home
To the place of parenting; yet in the throes of generation
It means nothing but a sudden curvetting in foam,
A salmon's leap to reach the head of the loch.

In the house of darkness, the poet muses long
Into the night. To no luminary constant, spurning
Sun, moon and stars, to come to the place of turning,
Where he dances solitary, far from the chiding throng.

WHEN ANCIENT STARLIGHT FALLS TO EARTH

Tracing the threefold spirals of the entrancing dark,
He is purely given, in the way of his kind, to the gifting
Cauldron, the utter source and centre where he births and dies.

Behind his sightless, all-envisioning, lightless eyes,
The vision crests in the embrace of the primal parents,

And there is only darkness shattered by shards of eternity.

# CLEAVE TO YOUR STAR

Now when the blessed night comes fast,
When every minute, like the flower, closes,
Bows its head before the glories past,
And timeless falls as scarlet-petalled roses,

Welcome the dimness that foretells the dark,
When voyagers in their wandering grazes
Silently approach the meadow's mark,
Still following their ancient mazes.

Dust that I am, behold the brightness far,
The Titans' dancing ground translated,
Descendent of a thousand, yet one star
That shines upon me—as I am related.

Tell me again, as once a wisdom known,
What story we have shared, belonging.
Wake in fierce memory, in brittle bone,
The song uncompassed by your calm be-thronging.

## WHEN ANCIENT STARLIGHT FALLS TO EARTH

'Cleave to your star,' night's dancers ever sing,
Sleep deeply in our starlight dreaming.
Your dust we stir and to the ages fling:
This is the story and its endless meaning.'

# ETERNALLY ENGRAVED

All we as dancers in our circlings round,
In imitation of the stars' own glory,
Seek out the Gods' own dancing ground,
As we attempt to tell their story.

We are not tablets unengraved, not blanks,
But books eternally unscrolling.
The writer writes us—though we give no thanks—
Sometimes we miss the soundless words' unrolling.

We learn, as in the twinkling of a dream,
But on awaking learning slips away:
As tides that turn from littorals marine,
Leaving the shore quite dry and we bewrayed.

Within us all the maker's seeds are sown,
Each sparkling grain, a world potentially remembered,
At first, a scintillation all unknown,
At last, an ancient knowledge reassembled.

# CHANT OF THE ANCESTORS

We are the stars in the earth
We will keep the spirit pure
We will bring the soul rebirth.

# POETIC CONTEXTS

## SONGS

*Brightest Stars:* is from my album *Deep Well in the Wildwood*. It is sung to the tune of the Gaelic song, *Maideanan na h'Airidh*. I have sung it at many funerals.

*Nehalennia the Steerswoman*: Nehalennia is the goddess of travellers and traders. She was worshipped in 2-3rd centuries CE in Gallia Belgica, specifically around the Domberg region of Zeeland in the Netherlands. In this chant, she is the one singing.

*Orkney Song*: I have been travelling to Orkney regularly since 1977. This expresses my wellbeing at residing in what archaeologically-speaking in 'Neolithic Central.'

*Sacred Companions*: is from my novel *Troytown Dances* and appears on my album *Deep Well in the Wildwood*. It a homage to the ancestors.

*The Hyperboreans*: is based upon Pindar's *Tenth Pythian Ode*. It expresses the quest for the heritage of ancestral wisdom of Britain which is undertaken by the soul.

*Troytown Song*: is from my novel *Troytown Dances* and also appears on my album *Deep Well in the Wildwood*. In the novel, this is the traditional song accompanying a Cornish labyrinth dance.

*Song of the Spheres*: appears on my album *Deep Well in the Wildwood*. It sings of the Spindle of Necessity, and its source can be found in the Myth of Er, at the end of Plato's Republic; and it also takes up hints from the Hellenic-Egyptian Hermetic text, *Kore Kosmou*.

## SEASONS

*Hearth Song*: this first appeared in my book *Fireside Stories,* published by Barefoot Books 2007.

*Snow-Day*: the reference to 'the kill-joy Scrooge-cop,' comes from an incident in the USA in 2015, when a group of teenagers threw snowballs at a cop and he responded by drawing his gun.

## OCCASIONS

*Dawn Watch*: first published in *The Black River: Death Poems*. My mother, Olivia Florence Woodward died just after dawn on 12 March 2008. As she stopped breathing. two birds flew up.

*Out of the Workhouse*: only my father and his sister knew that my paternal grandmother had been in the workhouse from the age of 4-13, with her mother, sister and brother, after they were abandoned by a step-father. The rest of the family learned about this from the funeral eulogy. Her courage in adversity still moves me.

*An Expostulation Upon AI*: this poem emerged from genuine anger at learning that many of my books had been scaped by an AI company 'to help model writing.'

*An Ode to Oxford Physicke*: this was written in 2021 on the occasion of the coming of the first Covid vaccine, AstraZenica, prepared by Oxford scientists. It first appeared in my online Plague Diary 2020-1, *Inadvertant Anchorite* where I wrote every day on Facebook to cheer everyone up. I wrote it as Chaucer might have experienced Covid, since he himself lived through the 14th century Black Death. Read it aloud and you will get it!

## LOVE

*Love's Invasion*: was written after my escape from a lamentable first marriage and the long illness that accompanied it.

*Beauty and the Beast*: the Psyche story found its lodging in folktale in this most engaging of stories. I love every rendition of it.

*I Will Be Your Bonny*: despite what I wrote in the preface, this song came with tune and words *on the way to* John's 70th birthday party at our friend Dwina's house in Thame. I just had time to finish it and sang it at the party.

*Within Kabbalistic Memory*: is from a longer sequence, *The Book of Lights*. It explores love in the context of the Kabbala's imagery of the tradition.

## MYTH

*Where Three Cranes Fly At Dawn*: this poem appears in my novel *Troytown Dances,* when one of the two major protagonists, the dancer Verney, is memorialised by his lover, the poet Miranda.

*The Myth is Yet Living*: written to repel the grotesque warping of the word 'myth,' which in our era has come to mean 'an untruth' or 'misassumption.' I still hold with the definition of the ancient world as the truest metaphorical remembrance, of essential matters, and with the saying of Sallustius, 'Myth is something that has never happened and is happening all of the time.'

*Minotaur*: this poem appears in my novel *Troytown Dances*.

*Essential Mythologies*: was also written in frustration at the leaching out of the mythic from our lives, and the betrayal, by the world of media, of the saving story that puts us back together when we have been broken by life.

*A Green Killing*: this is a poem of the Green Man. In the last section, remember he has his axe!

*Written in Gold*: this poem is a reworking of the Orphic initiates' road-map to the afterlife, as discovered in the tombs of initiates: these instructions were engraved upon small, rolled-up scrolls of gold about the necks of those who were initiates in ancient Greece.

*Arthur Wakens Everywhere*: This was written in response to an academic who assured everyone at a conference on Arthurian matters that 'King Arthur is just literature, not reality.' For so many people, these myths have kept the hope and inspiration running for centuries: I did not see why this person should spoil the road that keeps us steady.

*Survivors of Camlann*: There are several accounts that soldiers fighting for Arthur at the Battle of Camlann, which was a civil strife between himself and Medrawt (Mordred). The first account is found in *Culhwch and Olwen*:

- 'Morfran, son of Tegid (no one struck him in the battle of Camlann, by reason of his ugliness: all thought he was an auxiliary devil. hair had he upon him like the hair of a stag.)'
- 'Sandde Bryd Angel (no one touched him with a spear in the battle of Camlann because of his beauty; all thought he was a ministering angel.)
- 'And Cynwyl Sant (the third man that escaped from the battle of Camlann, and he was the last who parted from Arthur on Hengroen his horse.)

In another place, we find reports of more survivors:

'Here are the names of the men who escaped from the battle of Camlan: Sandde Bryd Angel (Angel's form) because of his beauty, Morfran ap Tegid, because of his ugliness, St Cynfelyn from the speed of his horse, St Cedwyn from the world's blessing, St Pedrog from the strength of his spear, Derfel Gadarn (the Strong) from his strength, Geneid the tall from his speed. The year of Christ when the battle of Camlan took place was 542' (pa. 13, 117b; quoted from *Yr Areithiau Pros* by David Hwenallt, p 90).

## DIVINITIES AND SPIRITS

*Daimonic Sequence*: I have been aware all my life of a daimon who directs my creative direction. He is a master of strict *arete*, as the Greeks would say. This is my homage.

*The Old Woman of Beare*: The Cailleach Beare is the ancient mountain Goddess of South West Ireland. A 9th century poem speaks of giving up everything to become a nun and regretting her youth. This poem also tells the other half of her story, as the inciter to passionate love. Her image remains over many church doors in the shape of the Sheila na Gig statues—grotesque and naked, she points to her own vulva as the true door by which we enter and leave life. (First published by Tambimuttu in *Poetry London,* Autumn 1979)

*Sovereignty's Challenge*: Sovereignty or *Flaitheas* is one of the Irish titles of the Goddess of the Land. It is she who tests the fitness of rulers, and also holds them to their task.

*Feast of the Queen of Snows*: this follows the theme of Sovereignty. Here the Goddess of the Land is in her winter form. I wrote it while flying home from Scotland.

# PRAYERS

*I Shall Take Poetry as my Prayer*: this is the prayer of Frithirs or Freers, the Scottish augurs whose job was to divine the season ahead. They stood barefoot on the threshold of the house, and fasting with eyes closed, to make the augury: whatever their eyes lighted upon became the sign of their prophecy. I have upkept this custom for the last 45 years and taught the way of it worldwide.

*Bone Song*: is part of the *Tomb of Eagle's Sequence*, and is about the Mesolithic horned cairn on South Ronaldsay on the Orkneys. Here the ancestors are speaking.

*Spell-Song to Restore the Earth*: from the *Orcadian Night Quartet*. I wrote this and its sister songs through one long summer night on Orkney. The Blessed Head refers to Bengideid Fran or Bran the Blessed, who, after a catastrophic attempt to rescue his sister Branwen from her Irish husband, returns wounded to Britain. He commanded that his head was to be cut off and buried at the White Mount (now the Tower of London) so that it might act as a defence against invasion. In this poem, by the dreams and stories that we tell, we restore the earth in a similar manner.

# PEOPLE

*Companions in Darkness*: Brian Keenan was one of the Lebanese hostages back in 1986-1990. Kept solitary and blindfolded most of the time, until moved into a cell with John McCarthy, he found himself talking to the spirit of the 18th century blind Irish harper, Turlough O'Carolan, who kept him sane during his captivity. He promised to be reciprocal with the harper, and wrote a biographical novel about him, called *Turlough* after his release. This companionship beyond time and space inspires and resonates strongly within me.

*The Lantern Bearer*: The novels of Rosemary Sutcliff shaped my childhood. When John and I last visited her, it was Candlemas, and her garden was covered with snowdrops and white doves. Her 1959 book, *The Lantern Bearers,* which won the Carnegie Medal, continues to furnish the best and most memorable quotation for those who feel that the world is going to ruin, and what might be our duty then:

> "I sometimes think that we stand at sunset,' Eugenus said after a pause. 'It may be that the night will come close over us in the end, but I believe that morning will come again. Morning always grows again out of the darkness, though maybe not for the people who saw the sun go down. We are the Lantern Bearers, my friend; for us to keep something burning, to carry what light we can forward into the darkness and the wind."—Rosemary Sutcliff, *The Lantern Bearers*

*He Was Made Music*: both Dylan Thomas and Gerard Manley Hopkins have had a profound impact upon my own poetry, because of their innate musicality. This homage to Thomas was originally written for a poetry competition but it went longer than the rules allowed. I tried to capture both his brilliant verse and self-sabotaging life-style as he rogued his way through a fore-shortened career.

*To Her Secret Bower*: although I was just born in the reign in the King

George VI, his daughter, Queen Elizabeth II reigned throughout my whole life, dying on 8th September 2022. The two French phrases express her duty: *Noblesse oblige* signifies the duty that nobility owes to those within their realm, wherein privilege is balanced by service, as her life was. As the news came in about her passing, social media trolls began to deride the monarchy, while others, fearful of sounding monarchist, expressed their faint sorrow. *Honi Soit Qui Mal Y Pense* is the motto of the Order of the Garter, the highest order of chivalry within Britain: it means 'shame to those who think ill of it.' The Lion and Unicorn are, of course, the heraldic supporters of the Royal Coat of Arms.

## PLACES AND JOURNEYS

*Farewell, You Bright Dancers*: first published in *Migrations*, edited by Simon R. Wilson. Menopause is a peculiar journey that all women take. It is undertaken across a trackless waste, with no map. I had always steered my creativity by its monthly rhythms, and then my cart began to lose its wheels. I regained creative momentum by steering instead by the phases of the moon as my new rhythm, whereby my dreams could find their road again.

*Beyond the Ninth Wave:* the ninth wave was considered anciently among the Celtic nations to be the place where one country finishes and where 'overseas' began. Malefactors were exiled 'beyond the ninth wave,' to the mercy of Manannán Mac Lir, god of the sea. Here I was packing for a trip to the Isle of Lewis with my friend Felicity Wombwell.

*Bhalasaigh Sunset*: this poem marks my first visit to the Isle of Lewis. You pronounce Bhalasaigh as Vall'as-say.

*Sea Master*: this beach-combing poem honours the lord of the sea himself, Manannán mac Lir. It is a sorrow to me that I live inland and equidistant from 3 seas.

*Bosham Sequence*: in February 2025, John and I chose to spend our 50th anniversary in Bosham, West Sussex—a county that we both know well. *A Quieting* is about Holy Trinity Bosham Church. *Harold Embarks* follows Harold Godwinsson who, as King of Britain fought at Senlac against William, Duke of Normandy in 1066: it refers to the oath that Harold swore, which the Normans saw as fealty to a future King of Britain, but which Harold doesn't seem to have believed in. *Canute's Daughter*; King Canute's (unnamed) daughter is believed to have been buried at Bosham Church after drowning in the millrace. I have conflated this with Canute's famous commanding of the waves to return. *Sea Ways* recalls Bosham harbour.

## VISIONS

*Sea-Lanterns*: Another beachcombing poem from Isle of Lewis where a single black stone told me its story. If all other employments were closed to me, I would make a champion beach-comber.

*In Praise of Darkness*: written to honour the artist, Thetis Blacker, this poem first appeared in Temenos II in 2008. It was inspired by a series of Thetis' massive batiks which adorned Winchester Cathedral in 1991.

*In Dazzling Darkness*: the ancient Gaelic poets composed in darkness, having been trained in the houses of darkness—darkened bothies—to follow metaphor in the darkness. This process of composition was a visionary one: here I have included the salmon's return journey to the source, and referenced the gifting cauldron which is a common image in pan-Celtic tradition. This tradition of darkness is one which I have instinctively followed all my life, since I was pre-verbal, pulling round me a blanket to exclude light to perceive vision in the darkness.

*Cleave to Your Star*: Plato tells us that we each have our own star, and I believe him. We are made of the dust of the stars, science tells us, confirming this understanding, though saying nothing about the Titans whose dust is scattered equally within us.

*Eternally Engraved*: this poem is inspired by Proclus whose vision is very close to my own.

*Chant of the Ancestors*: the end chant was given to me by the ancestors as I overflew Cincinati in the early 1990s. I have sung it all over the world with many students, a precious fragment and reminder that we are here for a while, and then reborn, depending on how well we honour our spiritual vision. We cannot sing it if there is any hubris in us.

# ABOUT THE AUTHOR

CAITLÍN MATTHEWS is the author of over 85 books, including *Celtic Book of the Dead* and *The Lost Book of the Grail*. Her poetry was published in *Poetry London* by the late Tambimuttu, and her first collection, *Search for Rhiannon* appeared in 1981. She is known internationally for her work on the mythic and ancestral traditions of Britain and Ireland. Caitlín is a co-founder of the Foundation for Inspirational and Oracular Studies (FÍOS), which is dedicated to the sacred arts that shape the landscape of the soul, via vision, dream and memory. She has a shamanic healing practice in Oxford. For books, events and courses, see www.hallowquest.org.uk

For new, regular writing, see https://hallowquest.substack.com

www.ingramcontent.com/pod-product-compliance
Lightning Source LLC
Chambersburg PA
CBHW031320160426
43196CB00007B/603